THE 3E METHOD
JOURNAL

33 Days to
Evoke, Embrace & Evolve

Insightful Journaling for
Personal Growth

LIZA BOUBARI

Best Selling Author of Stand Up to Slim Down

For authorized copies of this document, please contact HealWithin.com or (818) 551-1501. Enjoy reading

Print: 979-8-9925681-3-4
eBook: 979-8-9925681-4-1
LCCN: 2025908274

Published by HealWithin, Inc.
330 Arden Ave Suite 130
Glendale CA 91203
www.healwithin.com

DEDICATION

To every woman who has ever silenced her voice, buried her pain, or questioned her worth, this journal is for you. May these pages be a mirror for your truth, a sanctuary for your healing, and a guide to your transformation.

To the brave women walking through these uncertain yet extraordinary times—May you Evoke what was, Embrace what is, and Evolve into all you are meant to be.

To the young women and daughters coming into their own —May you know that your worth is inherent, your voice is powerful, and your presence is a gift. You are the light we've been waiting for.

And to the women who shaped me—my beloved grandmother and mother—Your strength, grace, and unwavering love are woven into every page. You are my foundation. You Matter.

Lovingly,

Liza

A MESSAGE FROM LIZA

As women, we journey through sacred transitions—girlhood to womanhood, into the sacred roles of motherhood, menopause, and beyond. Each stage holds its own wisdom, its own beauty.

So today, I invite you to pause and honor yourself. Say it with me: My body matters. What I feel matters. I matter.

Like the lotus, we may rise from muddy waters—pain, struggle, uncertainty. And still, we bloom. The lotus does not rush to the sun. It waits until it is ready. And when it is, it turns to the light with grace.

May this guide be your companion... a mirror for your truth... and a gentle nudge toward your own blossoming.

You are worthy. You are powerful. And yes—you matter.

With love,

Liza

INTRODUCTION

Welcome to your 3E Journal—a sacred space created just for you. By opening these pages, you are saying yes to healing, self-discovery, and to honoring the wisdom within you. This moment is no coincidence. You're here because something within you knows it's time.

True healing begins the moment you turn inward, not to fix what's broken, but to reconnect with what's always been whole. Through reflection, awareness, and intention, this journal is your companion in unveiling thoughts, emotions, and patterns that may have kept you feeling stuck or unseen.

Q: Are you interested in achieving your life's goal and dreams, or are you committed to achieving them? If interested, you will do what is comfortable and convenient. If you are committed, you will do whatever it takes! If you are committed, you'll start today!

Every prompt, every pause, every word you write is a step toward clarity, confidence, and inner peace. As you journey through these pages, you'll begin to recognize that healing isn't a destination; it's a daily practice of choosing you.

You already carry everything you need. This journal simply invites you to remember. So, breathe. Be still. And begin.

Lovingly,

Liza

EVOKE – WHAT WAS

Your past is not your enemy—it is the foundation upon which you stand. It holds the blueprint of your journey, woven with experiences, lessons, and choices—some made by you, others made for you. Instead of resisting it, feeling as if life was unjust or unfair, just for now, acknowledge it.

Look back, not to dwell, but to understand. Your history holds wisdom. Within these pages, you will gently explore your past—not as something to escape, but as something to learn from, grow from, and perhaps even honor.

Evoke

- Recognize the patterns that have influenced your life.
- Shift from resistance to awareness—own your history. Honor your past with compassion; it made you who you are.
- Extract the lessons that guide your next step forward.

EMBRACE – WHAT IS

Your present is where real change begins. Right here, right now—in this moment, you are enough. Just as you are.

This journal is an invitation to embrace your truth, without criticism or judgment. The choices you've made, the emotions you've carried, and the thoughts that shape you every day—are yours to observe, accept, and evolve from.

Here, you will meet yourself as you are and recognize the strength, tenacity, resilience, and beauty that have always been within you.

Embrace

- Accept where you are as a starting point, not a limitation.
- Choose how you respond to your circumstances—this is your power.
- Love yourself enough to stand in your truth, without judgment.
- Understand that awareness leads to transformation.

"It's not what heals you that matters –
what matters is how you heal within." ~Liza

EVOLVE – TO WHAT WILL BE

Your future is not written in stone—it is waiting for your dreams to create.

- Who do you choose to become?
- How do you desire to feel?
- What life are you stepping into?

You are no longer bound by your history or old narratives. With every reflection, every realization, every choice, and every commitment you make within these pages, you are evolving toward the life, the mindset, and the well-being you truly desire.

Transformation does not have to be drastic—it can be as simple as blossoming into the person you have always dreamed of becoming. You are worthy of growth, of love, of healing, of having the life you desire.

Evolve

- Set a vision for your future—clear and intentional.
- Take bold steps toward your desired lifestyle, mind, body, and emotions.
- Believe in yourself fully, because your dreams are valid.
- Recognize that transformation happens through consistent, empowered choices.

What were 3 Challenges of the week?

_____

_____

_____

What were 3 of my WINS for the week?

_____

_____

_____

TIME TO HEALWITHIN

Cultivate Positive Habits: Integrate uplifting journaling into your daily routine for lasting positive change.

Daily Reflection: Stay grounded, present, and in touch with your inner self through regular reflection.

Healing Through Writing: Release stress, worries, and daily concerns by putting pen to paper.

Mindful Self-Reflection: Slow down and gain a fresh perspective on your thoughts and experiences.

This self-care guide can serve as a foundation for personal development, promoting reflection and action toward self-growth and empowerment. Each page invites you to engage actively with the content and apply the insights into daily life.

Evoke What Was: Acknowledge and honor your past.
Embrace What Is: Accept and appreciate your present reality.
Evolve to What Will Be: Manifest and cherish your future self.
Because...You Matter.

A POWERFUL INVITATION

Before you continue in this journal, pause.

Take a selfie today. No filters. No touch-ups.
No expectations. Just you. As you are, in this moment.

As you move through these pages, pay attention. Notice
the shifts within you—the way your thoughts evolve,
how your emotions soften, the clarity that begins to
emerge.

On the last day, take another picture. Look at both.
What do you see? How do you feel?

Has your expression changed?
Has your posture softened?
Do your eyes shine a little brighter?
Is there a new sense of peace, confidence, or joy within
you?

This is what transformation looks like—not forced, yet
naturally unfolding from within.

Because You Matter.
When you believe in YOU, all possibilities become
reality.

Your past does not define you.
Your present empowers you.
Your future is yours to create—one word,
one reflection, one choice at a time.

PERSONAL DEVELOPMENT AND SELF-CARE

Personal development is a lifelong journey of growth that requires nurturing your physical, emotional, and mental well-being. Self-care is the foundation of personal development, enabling you to recharge and connect with yourself.

Key Concepts:

- Prioritize self-care practices like sleep, healthy eating, and physical activity.
- Engage in activities that bring joy, such as hobbies, meditation, or time with loved ones.
- Self-care isn't selfish—it's essential to growth.

Exercise:

List three self-care activities you can commit to daily. Identify one habit you can let go of that drains your energy.

Affirmation: "I nurture my mind, body, and soul with care, allowing myself to thrive in all areas of life."

BUILDING SELF-ESTEEM

Understanding Self-Esteem: Self-esteem is the value you place on yourself. High self-esteem encourages confidence, while low self-esteem can lead to doubt and self-criticism

Key Concepts:

- Identify and acknowledge your strengths.
- Celebrate small achievements.
- Let go of comparisons to others and focus on your unique essence.

Exercise:

Write down five qualities you admire about yourself. Recall a recent achievement and reflect on how it made you feel.

Affirmation: "I am worthy of love, success, and happiness. I recognize my value in every step I take."

EMBRACING SELF-ACCEPTANCE

What is Self-Acceptance?
Self-acceptance is the practice of embracing all parts of yourself, including flaws and imperfections. It allows for growth without the need for constant self-criticism.

Key Concepts:

- Accept where you are in your journey without judgment.
- Shift your focus from perfection to progress.
- Embrace both successes and setbacks as learning opportunities.

Exercise:

List three self-care activities you can commit to daily.
Identify one habit you can let go of that drains your energy.

 Affirmation: "I accept and appreciate myself fully as I am today, and I trust in my ability to grow and evolve."

MANAGING ANXIETY

Understanding and Managing Anxiety: Anxiety is a normal stress response, yet it can be overwhelming when it takes control. Learning to manage anxiety empowers you to face challenges with calm and clarity.

Key Concepts:

- Practice deep breathing exercises to calm the mind and body.
- Use mindfulness techniques to stay grounded in the present moment.
- Identify triggers and develop healthy coping mechanisms.

Exercise:

Create a "calm plan" for moments of anxiety: list 3-5 calming techniques (e.g., breathing exercises, journaling, or a brief walk).
Reflect on a recent anxious moment and how you can manage it differently next time.

Affirmation: "I am in control of my emotions, I can handle things better each day, and I choose peace and calm in every situation."

SILENCING THE INNER CRITIC

Overcoming the Inner Critic: The inner critic is the negative voice inside that doubts your abilities and belittles your efforts. Learning to quiet this voice is crucial for selfconfidence and personal growth.

Key Concepts:

- Challenge negative thoughts with facts and evidence. Ask yourself, "is this true?"
- Replace criticism with compassionate self-talk.
- Practice gratitude for your achievements, big and small

Exercise:

Write down three critical thoughts you've had recently. For each, write a positive counter-statement.
Reflect on how these positive statements make you feel compared to the critical ones.

Affirmation: "I release negative self-talk and replace it with kinder words of love and encouragement."

CREATING AND ENFORCING BOUNDARIES

The Importance of Boundaries: Setting healthy boundaries is essential for maintaining balance in relationships and protecting your energy. Boundaries allow you to prioritize your needs and well-being without guilt.

Key Concepts:

- Recognize when to say no and honor your limits. No is as OK an answer as yes.
- Set clear, respectful boundaries with others.
- Understand that boundaries are not selfish; they are a form of self-respect.

Exercise:

Identify a situation where you need to set a boundary. Write down how you will communicate it clearly and confidently.
Practice saying no in low-stakes situations to build your confidence in boundary-setting.

Affirmation: "I have the right to set healthy boundaries and to protect my energy and well-being."

WRITING YOUR NEW STORY

Crafting Your New Narrative: You have the power to rewrite your life story. By changing your internal narrative, you create a future that aligns with your desired goal and highest potential.

Key Concepts:

- Focus on where you want to go, not where you've been.
- Visualize your ideal self and how that person thinks, acts,
- and feels. Step into it!
- Take small, consistent steps toward your goals with
- confidence.

Exercise:

Write a brief story about your future self—what do you feel,
do, how do you live? What does your life look like one year from now? Be as detailed as possible.
Identify one action you can take this week to move closer to that future vision.

Affirmation: "I am the author of my own story, and I choose to write a life filled with purpose, joy, love, kindness, prosperous and success."

WRITING YOUR NEW STORY

Today's Date: _____

What is my

1. Emotional State
Mood: _____
Emotional Stability: _____
Stress Levels: _____

2. Thought Patterns
Positive Thoughts: _____
Negative Thoughts: _____

3. Physical Well-being
Energy Levels: _____
Physical Symptoms: _____

4. Behavior and Activities
Daily Activities: _____
Productivity:_____

5. Sleep Patterns
Sleep Quality: _____
Sleep Duration: _____

6. Self-care Practices
Self-care Activities: _____
Nutrition: _____

7. Coping Strategies
Stress Management: _____
Problem-solving: _____

8. Goals and Accomplishments
Goal Progress: _____
Achievements: _____

9. Mindfulness and Reflection
Mindfulness Practices: _____
Reflection: _____

10. Support System
Support Network: _____
Seeking Help: _____

11. Overall Well-being
General Satisfaction: _____
Purpose and Meaning: _____

When you shift how you felt then -
it shifts how you feel now. ~LizaB

Go through each section
On a scale of 1 to 10, how do you rate yourself -
10 being best.

Emotionally _____
Spiritually _____
Intellectually_____
Physically _____
Environmentally _____
Financially _____
Occupationally _____
Socially _____

DO SOMETHING
TODAY
THAT YOUR FUTURE
SELF WILL

"We must live in the joy of promise and recall that every human being has a unique perception and method of programming their world—until they decide to amend it." – Liza

I feel things I do not understand.

I can't find the words to express.

I just need someone to listen.

I miss the person I was.

I feel uncertain.

I am not where I thought I'd be.

I outgrow people and habits.

It's Ok if...

I plan on doing nothing.

I need to ask for help.

I am tired of giving and pleasing.

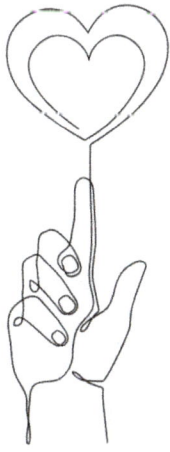

How Do I Feel Today?

1. Emotional and Physical Check-in

Emotionally: (Circle one or more)
o Happy
o Sad
o Excited
o Calm
o Angry
o Afraid
o Other: _____

Physically: (circle one or more)
o Energetic
o Tired
o Sick
o Healthy
o Sore
o Relaxed
o Other: _____

Mentally: (circle one or more)
o Exhausted
o Calm
o Excited
o Anxious
o Content
o Overwhelmed
o Other: _____

Gratitude
2. List three things I AM grateful for today:

_____

_____

_____

3. Top 3 Priorities
Identify my top three priorities for today:

_____

_____

_____

4. Positive Affirmations
Complete the following affirmations:

I am _____

I can _____

I will _____

I feel _____

5. Daily Accomplishments
What did I accomplish today?

_____

_____

_____

"Only do what your heart tells you."
- Princess Diana

6. Reflection: What Went Well?

_____

_____

_____

7. What can I improve for tomorrow?

_____

_____

_____

8. Self-Care Activities
How did I take care of myself today?

Eating healthy meals
Exercising
Meditating
Spending time with loved ones
Engaging in a hobby
Getting enough sleep
Other: _____

9. Daily Rating
Rate your overall day by circling one:

 Amazing!
Good
Okay
Could be better
Tough day

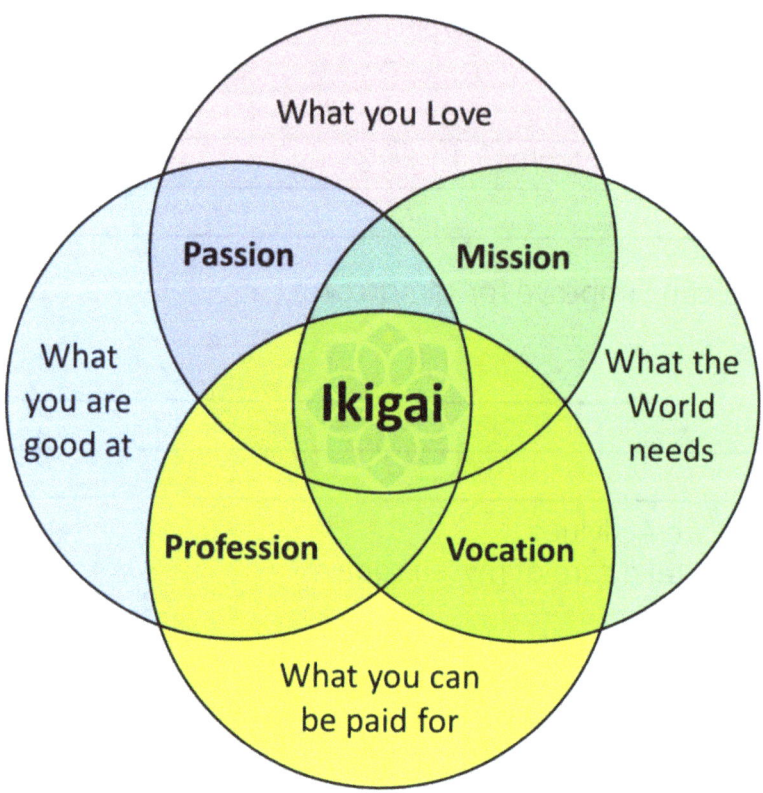

Ikigai is about finding joy, fulfillment, and balance in the daily routine of life.

The fundamental truth of Ikigai is that nothing is separate. Everything is connected.

Take a look at the four elements of the ikigai diagram: what you love, what you're good at, what the world needs, and what you can be.

WRITE DOWN YOUR WISH LIST (BUCKET LIST)

Your journal is an ideal canvas for crafting your bucket list.

Setting goals starts with capturing them in writing. When you jot down your aspirations, you lay the foundation for turning dreams into reality.

Create a list of experiences you want to have, places you long to visit, and goals you aim to achieve. Remember, if you can dream it, you can achieve it.

Embrace daydreaming as a powerful way to connect with your inner self. If visualization isn't your strength, imagine your dreams vividly.

Ask yourself:
- What brings me joy?
- What am I passionate about?
- What makes me smile?
- What would brighten my day?

Your journal is your personal blueprint for manifesting these dreams.

Your Journey: From Then to Now

Pause for a moment. Breathe.

You have arrived at this final page—not at an end, but at a new beginning.

Look back at where you started. The thoughts you carried, the emotions you explored, the truths you unveiled.

• What has shifted within you?
• What have you learned about yourself?
• How has your perception of your past, present, and future evolved?

This is not about judgment—this is about self-reflection. You are not measuring your worth or success, but acknowledging your growth. Brava to YOU!

You showed up for yourself. You turned inward. You honored your truth.
What do you celebrate about yourself today?
What words of encouragement would you give your past self?
What wisdom will you carry forward into your future?

Bravo!

Take one last look at your first journal entry.

Compare it to where you are now. Now, take a look at the two selfies—do you see the light within you?

✦ The way your eyes reflect your truth.
✦ The way your energy has shifted.
✦ The way your presence feels... more you.

This is transformation. This is you—stepping into who you are meant to be.

Your thoughts, body, emotions, spirit, and life matters.
Evoke, Embrace, Evolve ..."You Matter"

Everyday in every way,
I accept and appreciate myself for who I am.
I do Matter!

Liza's '33 Days' New Habit Forming Theory:

You may have heard the phrase "It takes 21 days to form a habit." Liza's philosophy is that it takes '33 consecutive days of repeating the same thing over and over, either good or bad, to change and form a new habit.

Are you wondering why 33 days instead of 21 days?
We as humans are creatures of habit and function in a society where everything is measured by "time." This means we know and understand seconds, minutes, hours, days, weeks, and months. Most days in a month are 30 or 31. So if we continue a new routine for over 33 consecutive days, then we have done it for over an entire month and are already into the next month. Follow me so far?

Most think and feel, "If I can do it for over a month, I wonder if I can continue it for the next 33 days," thus placing the new programming into action for the next month.

Simply put, instead of coming short in the month (21 days), you have now accomplished something you did not believe was imaginable. While your entire thought process was to do something for 33 days continually, the pressure and the discomfort of "possible failure" is lifted...and by the second month, your subconscious is already forming the new habit. Bingo!

You now create a new pattern of thoughts and conquer old habits. Saying to yourself: "I can do this" - "it works"! Success feeds success!
And what is "it"? IT is YOU.

DAY 1

What are your feelings right now?
(write till you shift from thinking to feeling)

- If my life were a movie, what would the overall message be - what is my story?
- What gets me excited and motivated?
- What do I stand for, feel passionate about, or deeply believe in?

DAY 2

Everything in life stems from self-esteem.

- What is my struggle through my journey that is bigger than me?
- What is something I am willing to fight for or love for?
- What gives me reason to wake up each day?

Day 3

Why is this YOUR passion?

What is my driving force or passion?

- Is this a book?
- Is this a cause?
- Is this a course?
- Is this a lifestyle?
- Is this my family?
- Is this a business?

DAY 4

What daily rituals do you have?

How do these rituals help me feel better
and more productive through my day?

- Wake up early
- Meditate.
- Walk - Exercise.
- Eat a healthy breakfast.
- Write in a journal.
- Call a loved one.

DAY 5

**Think of a habit or behavior you want to change.
Most of us don't make a change until it really
hurts us, or the rewards are so much greater.**

- What 3 words define the best of who I am?
- What is great about my life?
- What is my BIG why right now – what excites me.

Day 6

How do you describe your path of spiritual development to this point?

- What do I value most in my life?
- What qualities do I most love and admire about myself?
- Why?
- How have they served me?

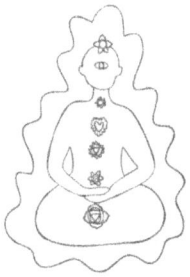

DAY 7

Dreams are the doorway to the soul.

- What is a recent dream I have had?
- What are the top 3 priorities in my life right now?
- Why are they important to me?
- How do I honor them?
- If I had all the courage and support, I would

"You have been holding the key to
your wellness and success all this time.
Now use it!" ~Liza

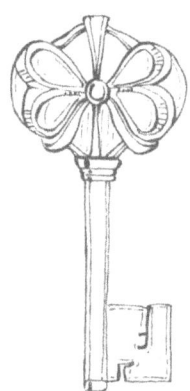

What were 3 Challenges of the week?

_____

_____

_____

What were 3 of my WINS for the week!

_____

_____

_____

DAY 8

Find a picture of yourself as a child - observe the picture.

- What did I dream about at that age?
- What were the highlights of my life - the lows?
- What are the lessons in each?
- Who or what drains my energy?
- What am I to do about it?

DAY 9

Recall a favorite memory.

- What does this memory remind me of?
- What makes this memory special?
- If I had a chance to trade places with one for a day, who would it be?
- How do I feel about this memory?

DAY 10

Think of a time that you were most courageous and emotionally strong.

- What strengths did I call upon?
- How has this experience influenced me?
- If I could alter or relieve an incident in my life, which would it be?
- What would I do differently?

DAY 11

What 3 words define how you engage and treat others?

- How do I view others?
  - ° Am I judgmental? Jealous? Helpful? Gracious?
- How may I serve others?
- How do I present myself to others?
- How would my life be different?

DAY 12

**How do you feel loved?
Do you know?**

- When did I first experience love?
- Who did I believe I loved first?
- What was it like?
- What does love mean to me now?
- How have my views on love changed over the years?

Do I feel loved today?
Do I know how to fully love another?
Do I love myself?

DAY 13

**Look back over your life, family,
or romantic relationships...**

- What patterns or themes can I identify?
- Who are the important people in my life?
- What do I admire or love most about them?

DAY 14

How have you grown over the last year?

- How is my life different compared to last year?
- What qualities have I developed to strengthen my character or life?
- Do I have qualities that I need to change for the better or develop further?
- If so, which qualities do I cultivate?

Every day in every way, I feel better than yesterday - but not as good as tomorrow!

What were 3 Challenges of the week?

_____

_____

_____

What were 3 of my WINS for the week!

_____

_____

_____

DAY 15

Here is a list of my favorite books, magazines.

- What do they have in common?
- Why were they interesting to me?
- What have I learned from them?

Day 16

What do I crave most?

- Am I aware when I eat?
- Do I eat because I'm hungry, or do I eat emotionally?
- What exactly do I crave?
    - Is it the food?
    - Am I stuffing my emotions?
    - Am I eating just to eat?
    - Am I hiding?
- The healthy and not-so-healthy way in which I comfort myself when I am upset, tired, or overwhelmed is?

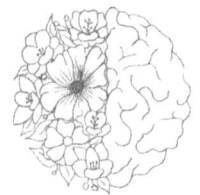

DAY 17

**Create an abundance list to see the blessings
you receive each day**

- How do I define success and abundance?
- What message did I learn growing up about money and wealth?
- How have these messages affected me in my adulthood?
- If I had all the money, time, confidence, and self-awareness in the world, how would my life be any different?
- Am I in a good place today?
- If not yet, what do I need to learn or do!

DAY 18

What is your perfect vacation?

- What is my memory of traveling as a child?
- Where would I love to travel to now?
- How would I go? With whom?
- What would I do - or want to experience?

DAY 19

What 3 boundaries do you need to set for yourself to create the space for more success in life - personally and professionally?

- What do I need for myself to feel more secure?
- How would I respond if someone were to ask me...
    - Who are you?
    - What do you want?
    - What more do you need?

DAY 20

As you decide to use your talents and gifts in an even greater way, what would you do differently?

- How do I show up in life?
- What are my strengths?
- What am I good at?
- What brings me joy?
- What do I want to project to others?
- How am I seen?

Day 21

What secrets have you been keeping that feel heavy on your heart?

- What am I holding on to?
- How has this been helping me?
- Is it even mine to keep or hold on to?
- What if I let it go?
- How will my life be better - how will I feel?

Write down your top 15 Skills -
Review the list and circle the ones
you resonate with most?

*"In the midst of darkness,
find your inner light."* ~Liza

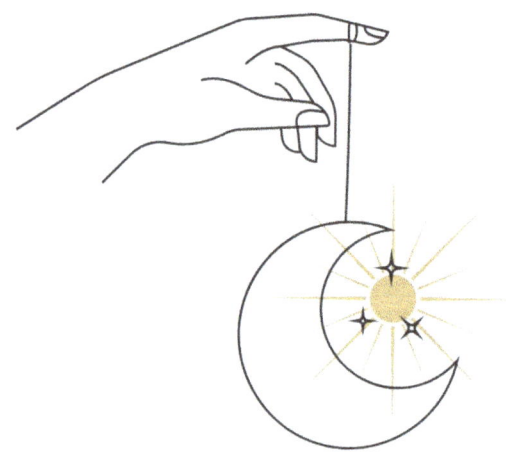

What were 3 Challenges of the week?

_____

_____

_____

What were 3 of my WINS for the week!

_____

_____

_____

DAY 22

Interview 3 close friends or family members - ask them to describe the qualities that make you unique and special.

- Am I willing and open to hear their honest opinion?
- What would they say?
- How do they see me?
- What are my not-so-good habits and traits?
- What did I learn differently about myself?

If I choose to, what is one change I am willing to do today! How would that change look like, sound like, feel like?

DAY 23

What do you dream about doing with your life?

- Is there anything stopping me?
- What more do I aspire to accomplish?
- What legacy do I wish to leave for others?
- What bigger impact do I want to make in life?

YES - I'm ready to feel it, I'm ready to see it,
I'm ready to BE it!
I Matter!

DAY 24

Write a letter to God, a Higher Power, or to your inner SELF

Dear....

I am writing this letter is to share my inner thoughts and deepest feelings...

This jourbal has made me realize ...

Here is what I have learned about myself ...

Here is my prayer ...

DAY 25

When your expectation is met, that becomes a true essence of who you are.

- Instead of making the best decision, I decide and take ownership of each decision.
- I realize this decision is the best decision for now.
- I allow myself to receive.
- I attract abundance into my life.

DAY 26

Pausing for a moment in life.

- I choose to slow down, to pause, and to enjoy the path I am on.
- The journey is as important as the destination.
- When I pause for a moment, I breathe for my body.
- I am thankful for everything that surrounds me.

DAY 27

Observe - write down 100 things you like or love that you have surrounded yourself with.

Here are all the things I have and surround myself with: List them.

_____
_____
_____

I can let go of things I no longer need. I can sell them, share them, or pass them forward and donate to charity.

I accept and appreciate myself for who I am. I am grateful for all I have. Confidence is defined as "I AM".

DAY 28

**Every experience has been a part of
your learning process?**

What experiences in my life can I:
- Appreciate
- Forgive
- See the lesson
- Let go of
- Be grateful to
- Keep and repeat!

Honor the ...
Lessons you were taught
Feelings you caught, and
Flowers you bought.

What were 3 Challenges of the week?

_____

_____

_____

What were 3 of my WINS for the week!

_____

_____

_____

Day 29

Everything you do is because of whatever you tried changing is no longer working.

- I stop fighting nature, I embrace it.
- It doesn't matter when I start the 33 days, I will follow along.
- I embrace change and the process.
- Nothing in life happens without grace.
- I appreciate this process of becoming.

DAY 30

Your Health is Your Wealth!

What small or major changes must I make to feel healthier...
- Mentally
- Emotionally
- Physically
- Financially
- Spiritually

How will these changes make me feel?

DAY 31

**I am excited and ready to immerse myself
and evoke my desired goals!**

YES - I'm ready to ...

- I See it
- I Feel it
- I Become It
- I Know it
- It - is ME!

I am Clearing, Composing, and Creating my desired lifestyle.

DAY 32

Breathing through...

- I now understand that the world is within me.
- I can be at peace with myself.
- I make room for more joy.
- I can enjoy life.
- I am the master of my feelings.
- I can be protective of my boundaries.
- I am worthy of a healthier life.
- I believe in the Gifts within me.
- I Matter!

DAY 33

Some meditate with their eyes closed, chanting a mantra, or eyes open and being mindful.

I meditate with my eyes open because - All is Right here.
- No words are necessary.
- Being present with myself is rewarding in itself.
- I am more conscious of my wants, needs, and desires.
- I am Safe with Me - in my Body
- I feel complete and content Being Me
- I can Heal Within

I know - I Matter

"Keep the Best - Dump the rest!" ~Liza

What were 3 Challenges of the week?

_____

_____

_____

What were 3 of my WINS for the week!

_____

_____

_____

I Did It!

I Matter!

YOUR JOURNEY CONTINUES...

This is not the end—this is just the beginning of a deeper, more empowered version of you.

If this journey has inspired you, I invite you to continue exploring:

- Expand Your Growth – Discover more books designed to guide you through healing, empowerment, and transformation.
- Experience Deeper Healing – Access guided audio recordings to help you relax, reset, and realign with your highest self.
- Work With Me – If you're ready to go deeper, I invite you to book a private session with me. Together, we'll unlock the clarity, confidence, and breakthroughs you are seeking.

THOUGHTS ARE LIKE RIVERS!

LET THEM FLOW!

www.HealWithin.com – Explore private sessions, workshops, daily affirmations, and healing resources.
www.LizaBoubari.com – Learn more about my books, audios, and speaking engagements.

"It's not what you eat –
but what's been eating at you."
Acknowledge it, Accept it, Allow it to go. ~Liza

ABOUT THE AUTHOR

Liza Boubari is a Motivational Speaker, Best-selling Author and Clinical Hypnotherapist with over 25 years of experience in mind-body healing. She is the founder of HealWithin, where she has helped thousands transform their lives by addressing emotional pain, stress, and limiting beliefs.

Liza's Boubari 3E Method—Evoke, Embrace, Evolve— empowers individuals to acknowledge their past, accept their present, and step confidently into their future. With a background in the corporate world, massage therapy, and a personal healing journey, Liza combines mind-body healing with practical tools for better and healthier change.

As the host of HealTalk Tuesdays and Real-Talk with Liza, (a radio show on AM870), she brings actionable insights to inspire audiences globally.

Through this journal, Liza invites you to step toward healing, growth, and in-depth exploration of your inner thoughts and self-reflection for the life you deserve.

Be sure to subscribe to Liza's YouTube channel for more empowering content, and explore her other books and audio recordings to continue your journey of self-discovery and healing.